Watch It Grow

A Turtle's Life

Nancy Dickmann

Heinemann Library
Chicago, Illinois

www.heinemannraintree.com

Visit our website to find out more information about Heinemann-Raintree books.

To order:

☎ Phone 888-454-2279

▣ Visit www.heinemannraintree.com to browse our catalog and order online.

Edited by Nancy Dickmann, Rebecca Rissman, and Catherine Veitch
Designed by Joanna Hinton-Malivoire
Picture research by Mica Brancic
Production by Victoria Fitzgerald
Originated by Capstone Global Library Ltd
Printed and bound in China by South China Printing Company Ltd

15 14 13 12 11 10
10 9 8 7 6 5 4 3 2 1

Library of Congress Cataloging-in-Publication Data
Dickmann, Nancy.
  A turtle's life / Nancy Dickmann. -- 1st ed.
    p. cm. -- (Watch it grow)
  Includes bibliographical references and index.
  ISBN 978-1-4329-4231-1 (hc) -- ISBN 978-1-4329-4234-2 (pb) 1.
Turtles--Life cycles--Juvenile literature. I. Title.
  QL666.C5D53 2011
  597.92--dc22
                              2010000092

Acknowledgments
We would like to thank the following for permission to reproduce photographs: Alamy pp. **4** (© P-59 Photos), **8** (Rolfnp/© Derrick Hamrick), **15** (© Gay Bumgarner), **22 top** (Rolfnp/© Derrick Hamrick); Corbis p. **14** (© David A. Northcott); FLPA p. **19** (Tony Hamblin); Getty Images p. **18** (Photographer's Choice/Joseph Devenney); iStockphoto pp. **7** (© Roger Whiteway), **11 inset** (© Brandon Laufenberg); Nature Picture Library pp. **6** (© Lynn M. Stone), **9** (© Lynn M. Stone), **12** (© Rod Williams), **11 main** (© Lynn M. Stone), **22 bottom** (© Rod Williams), **23 middle bottom** (© Lynn M. Stone); Photolibrary pp. **5** (Juniors Bildarchiv), 10 (Animals Animals/Allen Blake Sheldon), **13** (Juniors Bildarchiv), 16 (Animals Animals/Lynn Stone), **17** (Animals Animals/CW. Schwartz), **20** (Animals Animals/Joe McDonald), **21** (Animals Animals/Zigmund Leszczynski), **22 left** (Juniors Bildarchiv), **22 right** (Animals Animals/Allen Blake Sheldon), **23 bottom** (Juniors Bildarchiv), **23 middle top** (Animals Animals/CW. Schwartz), **23 top** (Animals Animals/Allen Blake Sheldon).

Front cover photograph of a box turtle reproduced with permission of Photolibrary (Peter Arnold Images/Ed Reschke). Inset photograph of a box turtle hatching reproduced with permission of Photolibrary (Animals Animals/Allen Blake Sheldon). Back cover photograph of a turtle hibernating reproduced with permission of Photolibrary (Animals Animals/CW Schwartz).

We would like to thank Nancy Harris for her help in the preparation of this book.

Every effort has been made to contact copyright holders of material reproduced in this book. Any omissions will be rectified in subsequent printings if notice is given to the publisher.

Contents

Life Cycles

All living things have a life cycle.

A box turtle has a life cycle.

egg

A turtle hatches from an egg.

It grows up.

egg

A turtle lays eggs. Later it will die.

Eggs and Hatchlings

nest

A female turtle lays eggs in a nest.

Each egg has a baby turtle inside.

Soon the baby turtle hatches from the egg.

nickel

The baby turtle is about the size of a nickel.

Young Turtles

The young turtle grows slowly
every year.

The turtle's shell grows, too.

worm

The turtle eats worms and insects.

The turtle eats fruits and roots.

Hibernating

The turtle hibernates all winter long.

The turtle makes a nest and rests.

Becoming a Turtle

The female turtle is ready to have babies.

The female turtle looks for a safe place to dig her nest.

The female turtle lays eggs in
the nest.

The life cycle starts again.

Life Cycle of a Turtle

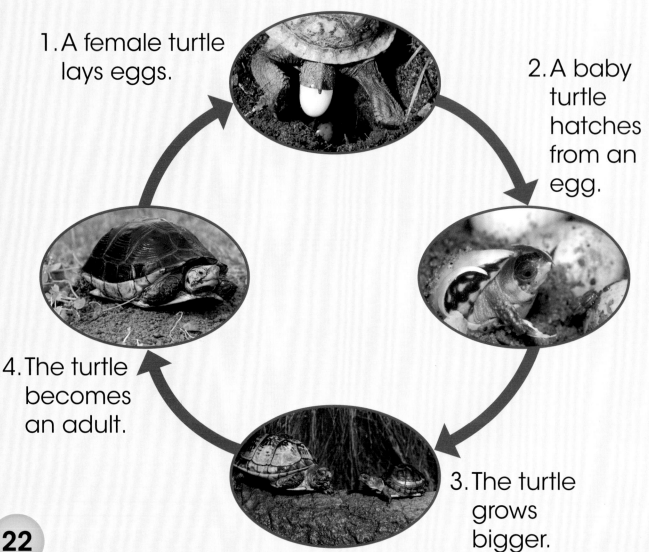

1. A female turtle lays eggs.

2. A baby turtle hatches from an egg.

3. The turtle grows bigger.

4. The turtle becomes an adult.

Picture Glossary

 **hatch** to be born from an egg

 **hibernate** to rest through the winter

 **nest** safe place where a female animal lays eggs

 **shell** hard covering that protects some animals

Index

Note to Parents and Teachers

Before reading

Show children a chicken's egg. Ask them if they know what it is called, and what animal it came from. Then encourage children to make a list of other animals that lay eggs. Tell children that turtles lay eggs, and that baby turtles grow inside. Then explain that all living things have life cycles, and that the turtle has a special life cycle.

After reading

· Explain to children that shells are a type of body covering. Explain that shells are a body covering that protect an animal's body. Use the images on pags 10–13 to show children how turtles' shells grow along with the turtles.

· Explain to children that many animals hibernate through the winter. They do this to save energy and stay protected from the weather. Ask children if they can think of any other animals that hibernate.